G000152512

Heresy

by
Fr Jerome Bertram

*All booklets are published thanks to the
generous support of the members of the
Catholic Truth Society*

CATHOLIC TRUTH SOCIETY
PUBLISHERS TO THE HOLY SEE

Contents

What is a Heresy?

A heresy is an erroneous opinion on some matter concerning God, ourselves, and how we relate to each other, taught in such a way as to undermine the Faith of the Church and draw people away from the Church. By origin, the word *heresy* derives from a Greek word meaning to pick and choose: it is being selective among the teachings of the Church and saying, "I will accept this point but not that one"; it is also being selective among members of the Church and saying, "I will accept these people and not those". Heresy nearly always involves *schism*, dividing the Church. The leader of a schism usually begins by teaching some erroneous opinion of his own, a heresy, and then declaring that those who do not accept it are not really Christians, so he leads his followers out into a schism, a new "denomination". The true heretic is one who has such an exalted opinion of his own ideas that he is prepared to insist on teaching them and spreading them, even against the united teaching of the universal Church; such an exalted opinion of his own importance that he aims at being the leader of a church of his own invention, rather than a faithful member of the Body of Christ. Those who follow him, if they think about the matter at all, can also be called heretics; those who are born into a schismatic and heretical body naturally cannot be blamed for it, and should not be called heretics, but encouraged to search for the truth.

Does Heresy matter?

The common opinion is that heresy does not matter, and that it is wrong and uncharitable to attempt to oppose heresy. The modern world unites around the opinions of the eighteenth-century in condemning the "intolerance" of those who attempt to eradicate heresy and heal schisms. The root of this "modern" idea (only three hundred years old) is that all theological statements are merely prejudices, born of inner feelings that are not subject to any rational analysis, and that to say one is wrong and the other right is as absurd as to say that it is wrong to like strawberries and right to like raspberries. Religious opinions, in the common view, are purely a matter of personal preference, and may be cheerfully tolerated as long as they themselves do not become intolerant. This idea derives from the philosophers and historians of the eighteenth century, who had the nerve to call themselves the "Enlightenment", and who ended up teaching that all religions and ideas may be tolerated except the Catholic Church. The eighteenth-century

"Enlightenment" led directly to the worst excesses of the French Revolution, when thousands of priests, nuns and lay Catholics were massacred in the name of "reason".

The word "terrorist" was coined to refer to the incorruptible Robespierre and his enlightened scientific philosophical comrades. It is now more familiar in the context of someone whose religious opinions lead him to kill and maim indiscriminately. Since 11th September 2001 the world can hardly say that religious opinions do not matter. We know that there are religious teachers whose doctrine includes the message that God requires and rewards slaughter and bloodshed on the heroic scale. All Muslims of my acquaintance agree that the teachers who promote terrorism like this are "heretics" in terms of Islam, leaders of "schisms" that draw people away from the true path. But then the teachers concerned probably think all my Muslim acquaintances are heretics in their turn. It is for the Muslims to deal with Islamic heresies: as Christians our task is to deal with ours. And if there are at present no Christian heretics who are spreading murder and mayhem on a large scale, that does not rule out the possibility: indeed the uneasy peace in Uganda with the so-called "Lord's Resistance Army" reminds us that terrorism can indeed spring from the bosom of the Catholic Church, fuelled by heretical ideas.

Perhaps a more familiar "heresy" preached until very recently by some denominations is the doctrine of racial superiority. Darwin taught the world to believe that all species, including mankind, have evolved, and that the process of evolution inevitably means the survival of the fittest. It is therefore the privilege and the duty of the fittest form of humanity to hasten the extinction of lesser sub-species. The full horror of this doctrine was seen in the fires of Auschwitz, but it was actively promoted in many apparently civilized countries where members of minority "races" were systematically sterilized to prevent their continuance. In South Africa, the much-reviled system of *apartheid* was only the logical outcome of the idea that one race, the "white", was further evolved and therefore superior to the "coloured" and the "black".

Conscience

The world agrees to repudiate racism and terrorism. But the world has no objective scientific grounds for doing so. The repudiation is based simply on natural feeling, the ingrained idea that certain things are wrong. Racism is wrong, terrorism is wrong, eating people is wrong. But why do people think like that? The answer is very simple: it is that "every human creature has by nature a *conscience*." (J.H. Newman)

And conscience is something that can only be explained in *theological* terms. Catholic theology can very easily explain why terrorism and racism and such horrors are wrong. Everyone else has to rely on instinct, which, as Newman pointed out, is simply the working of conscience without us knowing it. That instinct is so strong that modern societies will use every means, including violence, to oppose the theological errors or *heresies* which cause racism or terrorism. Conscience, even if unformed and unsure of its grounds, can be a force so strong that people will act on it without bothering to investigate whether there are rational grounds for their actions. But it is only theology that can tell us precisely *why* it is wrong.

Instinctive reaction to the dimly perceived voice of Conscience usually guides the majority of people to a correct appreciation of right and wrong. But a coherent rational synthesis of ideas can give us a better and clearer guidance. The synthesis of human experience with logical thought, with the data revealed through the teaching of Jesus Christ, and the voice of conscience, set out systematically with due consideration for possible objections, and careful analysis of different interpretations of the same data, is what the Catholic Church calls Theology. *And there is no other body on earth that even claims to have such a systematic coherent theology*. All other theologies at some stage include the acceptance of the irrational, a leap in the dark which does not integrate with the knowledge surrounding it.

Contradiction of official Catholic theology is what we call heresy: let us look at some examples.

Heresy concerning the Nature of God

If *theo-logy* means talking about God, heresy usually begins by talking about Him in the wrong way. The most obvious mistake is to think that there are many gods, but greater problems are caused if we fail to observe the distinction of persons within the One God. It took the combined wisdom of the greatest teachers of the Church over three hundred years to arrive at a satisfactory way of describing God, so we can hardly be expected to do it for ourselves in one lifetime. The hallowed formula, One God in Three Persons, was worked out by looking at all the alternatives and seeing how inadequate they were.

The most elementary of the mistakes is *polytheism*, the belief that there are many gods and goddesses and demi-gods of various sorts, all conceived very much in the image and likeness of man, with the same vices and jealousies and even the limitations of men. Such were our ancestors before St Augustine came to Kent and St Wilfred to Sussex; such are many people today. But we do not call them "heretics", for this is a pre-Christian belief, not a deviation from known truth.

The Gnostics

A variety which usually has been called a heresy is the idea that there are two equal and opposite gods, one who created and controls spirit, and is fundamentally good, and the other who created and controls matter, and is intrinsically evil. The idea was popular in Africa in the fourth century under the name of *Manicheeism*, and surfaced again in the Balkans in the twelfth century, spreading to the south of France, producing strange sects called *Bogomils*, *Cathars* or *Albigensians*. The root idea is known as *Dualism*, from the starting point that there are two gods. The French tourist board is keen to promote the memory of these heresies, on the principle that any enemy of the Catholic Church must be a good thing, but it seems odd in France to praise those who condemned both cooking and sex. The Manichees considered that the human body is utterly evil, and therefore that any use of the body is sinful. Those who were enrolled as "the Perfect" were committed to total sexual abstinence, and to strict vegetarianism, not because they loved animals but because they hated them, not because they valued sexuality in marriage as a holy sacrament, but because they believed marriage to be wicked. The Catholic Church continues to affirm the intrinsic goodness of all creation, for "God saw all that He had made, and behold it was very good". (*Gn* 1:31)

Manicheeism is actually only one of a group of heresies that claim to have a more perfect knowledge of God than is available to ordinary people. This idea crops up from time to time, that the real secrets about God are handed down from generation to generation in a small elite group, who are "perfect" or "knowing", while the ordinary run of the mill Christians and their clergy are kept in ignorance of the truth. These heresies are usually called *Gnostic*, from the Greek for "to know", because their devotees claim to know something the rest of us do not. When you penetrate their "secrets" they always turn out to be the most incredible rubbish: but what is more incredible is that Christ deliberately set out to deceive us by sending out his apostles with one version of the truth, while telling another version to the elite group. There are no secrets in Catholic teaching: but Our Lord did warn us against false teachers claiming to speak in His name. (*Mk* 13:5-6)

Arianism

Today various forms of *Unitarianism* and *Pantheism* have become more common than dualism or polytheism. The radical assertion that there is only One God can be distorted. In the fourth century the Church had to consider the various heresies which are grouped together under the term *Arianism*. Arius himself began with the fundamental principle of the unity of God, and therefore

taught that Jesus Christ could not really be God by nature.
Instead he claimed Jesus was a created being, like an
angel only higher, and "there was a time when he was
not." Others developed this theme, saying that Jesus was
of a "similar nature" to God, or was "like" God, or even
"unlike God". For decades these ideas were tossed about
in popular conversation as well as in the lecture room and
the pulpit, and the Roman Emperors took sides with
violence, imagining that they knew something about
theology. Eventually the voice of the ordinary people
prevailed, for they knew and loved Jesus Christ as truly
God, and they knew also the working of the Holy Spirit
as God in their lives. Great thinkers like St Athanasius,
St Basil and St Gregory helped formulate the faith of the
people, and the familiar words of the Nicene Creed were
accepted as the faith of the Church: Jesus is "God from
God, light from light, true God from true God, of the
same nature as the Father", and the Holy Spirit also is
"Lord and giver of life...together with the Father and the
Son adored and glorified." The phrase "of the same
nature" (*homo-ousios* in Greek) became the touchstone of
true belief. Since then Catholic Christians have been
happy to worship One God in Trinity, although it must be
admitted that the Arians survived as a separate
denomination for another two centuries and more, until
the regions they inhabited, North Africa and Spain, were

conquered by Muslims, and Arianism did not have the capacity to resist.

Unitarianism

Unitarianism, the idea that only the Father is God and that Jesus Christ and the Spirit are not, reappeared in Europe in the seventeenth century. The Protestants had repudiated the whole theological synthesis which made sense of the preceding Catholic development of doctrine, so people did not have the intellectual tools to examine these questions, and fell back on a simple, but inadequate, answer. Two strands diverged: the *Deists* believed in a single creator god, the "blind watchmaker", who started the world going, with its surrounding planetary systems, and then left us to get on with it, taking no further part and not interacting with creation at all. From this it is a simple step to *Atheism*, dispensing with the god concept altogether, and accepting the world as a self-explaining phenomenon. True atheists are actually extremely rare, a protected species that can only survive in an academic environment; most of the so-called atheists of the twentieth century believed in a supreme force called "History" which worked itself out in human affairs through a process of dialectic. But once we get to atheism and dialectical materialism, we have again moved beyond the confines of Christianity and cease to call them "heresies".

Pantheism

The other strand from Unitarianism is *Pantheism*, the belief in one all-encompassing god (or usually goddess) who comprises all that is, the sum total of all nature, human and animal, vegetable and mineral. Jesus Christ is, therefore, god, but no more so than you or I; the "god-self" expresses herself through each one of us in different ways, and the various stories we tell to convey that expression are all equally valid aspects of the One. This may be said to have become almost the majority religion in the modern West, but yet again it has moved beyond the confines of Christianity – indeed it explicitly and angrily rejects Christianity – and so must called a different religion, not a heresy.

What all these misconceptions of God have in common is that they make redemption through Jesus Christ meaningless, as we shall see on pages 21-26.

Heresy concerning the Nature of Christ

Speaking of God in Trinity, we inevitably come to look again at the Person of Jesus Christ. "Who do men say that I am?" (*Mt* 16:15) If it took over three hundred years to develop the doctrine of the Holy Trinity, it took another century to get a correct understanding of the nature of Christ, and this time the spun-off heresies turned out to be more enduring.

Not a man

In the very earliest days, in the lifetime of the Apostle John, there were people who denied "that Jesus Christ has come in the flesh". (1 *Jn* 4:2-3) They are known as *Docetists*, from the Greek word meaning "to seem", claiming that He really is God, but has no human nature, He only *seemed* to be human. Ancient primitive religions were very familiar with the idea that one of the gods might turn up on earth pretending to be one of us – Jupiter was always doing this, usually in the hope of meeting a human woman. The Jews were well aware that an angel could give a very plausible imitation of a human being (as in the book of Tobit). For Jesus to be God in disguise, or even an angel in disguise, was an easy idea to

understand. The idea dies hard: there are still many who
are uneasy with the concept that Jesus Christ is a real
human being just like us, but are perfectly capable of
believing He is divine. St John knew Him well, he was a
close relation, who heard Him, saw Him, touched Him (1
Jn 1:1), and he is so appalled by the idea that Jesus was
not human that he calls it the ultimate rebellion, the
Anti-Christ. For if Jesus is not really one of us, then He
was only pretending to share our life, only pretending to
eat and drink, only pretending to suffer and die. And that
means He was only pretending to love us.

Not God

The opposite idea, that Jesus was simply an ordinary human
being and no more, is surprisingly rare in the history of the
Church. It is know as *Ebionism*, from the Hebrew for "the
poor", but never really caught on before modern times. In
practice many of the later Arians may have simplified their
teaching to think of Jesus as a mere man, but usually people
felt instinctively that He is more than man. The modern
variation takes the line that Jesus was a perfectly harmless
Jewish rabbi, who never said or did anything out of the
ordinary, but was recognized as a very good man. They go
on to claim that all the stories about miracles are obviously
fraudulent, as are all the words attributed to Jesus which
indicate that He claimed to teach with the authority of the

Son of God. These additions, they say, were invented out of mistaken affection by those whose memories of Him had become blurred through the long ages before the gospels were written down. "Biblical critics" attempted to filter out all this pious embroidery to discover the original Jesus of Nazareth underneath. In the process, they left us virtually nothing of the Gospel of St John (which they prefer to call "the fourth gospel" to deny that was written by an eye-witness) and not much of the other three. Unfortunately for these "Biblical critics", more objective scholarship has shown that the Gospels are considerably earlier than they like us to think, well within the lifetime of eye-witnesses, and there is no historical evidence whatsoever for a "primitive" tradition of Jesus as a mere devout rabbi. Indeed, if He was no more than a perfectly harmless Jewish rabbi, who never said or did anything out of the ordinary, why on earth did anyone want to kill Him and persecute His followers? The "Jesus the simple Jew" heresy derives only from the wishful thinking of those who had already lost faith and wanted to justify their position. But it goes closely with "modernism" to which we shall return in the last section.

Nestorianism

Refinements of the two basic and obvious errors, Ebionism and Docetism, developed in the fifth century, with the equal and opposite heresies of *Nestorianism* and

Monophysitism. Nestorius was Archbishop of Constantinople, and first attracted attention when he denounced the familiar way of referring to Mary as the "Mother of God" (*Theotokos* in Greek). He meant to affirm that she was the mother only of the human nature of Jesus, not of the divine nature of the Second Person of the Trinity. His Catholic opponents agreed that the term is paradoxical, but insisted that it is valid, because it really drives home the truth that Jesus is a single person, both God and man. Nestorius himself seems to have become very muddled about what exactly he did mean, but his followers firmed their position into effectively denying that Jesus is a single person. There is one person, Jesus the son of Mary, who is a human being just like us, and there is another Person, the divine Word who somehow lives in him and speaks through him. This is not very different from saying that Jesus was a prophet, a man through whom God speaks. Nestorianism was roundly put in its place at the Council of Ephesus (431), but much of the Middle East broke away from the Church and set up a separate Nestorian denomination, largely for political reasons. It survives in many places, but since it had no effective answer to Islam, the majority of Nestorian Christians cheerfully accepted the new Prophet, and have moved out of the category of Christian heretics into that of members of a different religion. (Nestorius himself muttered that the teaching of the Council of Ephesus was what he had been trying to say all along. He was "wrong, but romantic": his opponent St Cyril was undoubtedly "right, but repulsive".)

St Cyril, Archbishop of Alexandria, the great, but sometimes harsh opponent of Nestorius, died soon after the Council of Ephesus, and his followers began to take his ideas to extremes. They produced what is called the *Monophysite* heresy: the idea that the human and divine are so fused in the one person of Jesus Christ that He has but a single nature. It was pointed out that this left Him neither really human, nor really divine, but something in between, and the Council of Chalcedon (451), with the help of Pope Leo the Great, produced the ideal definition, that Jesus is True God and True Man, one person in two natures. The Monophysites, again largely for political reasons, broke away to form a separate denomination. Since most were in Coptic Egypt, they became known as *Copts*, while the orthodox were called *Melkites*, the "King's Church", because they remained in communion with the Emperor. The Copts have greater resistance to Islam, but their isolation from the mainstream of Christianity has left them perilously weak in the face of pressure.

Most Christians were happy with the understanding taught at Chalcedon, and only minor heresies emerged later regarding the nature of Christ. One was the inevitable by-product of a well-meaning attempt to reconcile Copts and Melkites, producing a compromise formula that Jesus had only one will, though two natures, the *Monothelite* heresy. It did not catch on. A major disruption in the church in the later first millennium was the *Iconoclast* heresy, which was an aspect of docetism, and denied that any representation of the human form of Jesus could legitimately be made. Images or *icons* of Jesus and the saints were destroyed, and those who treasured them slaughtered. The eventual "triumph of Orthodoxy" was an affirmation that material things, such as icons, could be a real help in prayer, and that they did legitimately represent the human form of Christ, as of the saints. The Holy Spirit, too, has appeared in bodily form, and therefore this form can be represented.

Heresy concerning our own salvation

If we are wondering why it matters so much whether we are accurate in our assessment of the nature of God, or of the person of Jesus Christ, the answer is that it has a bearing on our own salvation, to the extent that if we get our understanding of God and Christ wrong, we destroy our own hopes of happiness in this world and the next.

This is because the whole point of Christianity is that it is only in Jesus that God delivers us from sin and death, and opens to us the possibility of eternal life. Why? Because we are "to share in the divinity of Christ, who humbled himself to share in our humanity." (text of the Mass, derived from St Athanasius, *De Incarnatione*) We find our link to God the Creator in the fact that Jesus, the Son of God, who is of one substance with the Father, came to share our common human nature, as true man. If He is not true man, then we have no real identity with Him. If He is not truly God, then our common nature with Him leaves us still utterly distant from God.

Pelagianism

If we do not have this link through the humanity of Jesus to his Divinity, then we are on our own in our efforts to break free from the limitations of this mortal life. This leads straight into the most common of all heresies, that of *Pelagianism*. Whether or not the original Pelagius taught it, the idea is that Jesus simply gives us a good example, and a code of conduct to live by, but it is up to us to model our conduct in such a way that we can defeat evil in our own lives and make ourselves fit for heaven. Pelagianism can of course do without Jesus altogether, for the code of conduct and the good example of any other religious teacher will do just as well. Pelagianism relies on a sense of our own self-importance, and natural pride: we can sort our own lives out. Sacraments become irrelevant: they may be useful ceremonies to show people how well we are doing, but have no use in themselves. The Church loses its importance: it becomes only a club of like-minded people anxious to congratulate each other on having sorted their own lives out. Redemption and salvation become redundant concepts. Many trends in modern "theology" fall into this category, without of course acknowledging the label "Pelagian".

The trouble with Pelagianism is that it just doesn't work. If we think that we can make ourselves perfect by our own efforts, using the Gospels simply as instructions in morality, we will certainly fail. I know, I've tried. Even if we could succeed in eradicating all the less desirable and socially unacceptable elements in our characters, we would be left with insufferable pride, which is of course by far the worst of all sins. And worse still, our modern neo-Pelagians don't even recognize how perilous pride is, in fact they think pride is a good thing. Which is why they have no sense of humour.

Pelaginanism essentially denies that we need help. That help is what we call *grace*. God gives us grace, He gives us Himself; He takes the initiative. Without God's action, we are trapped in a world where life is nasty, brutish and short. God takes the initiative in rescuing us from the world we have messed up for ourselves, and that initiative is focussed by the Church in the doctrines of the *Immaculate Conception* of Mary, and the *Virginal Conception* of Jesus. People love to mix up these two terms! By the Immaculate Conception we mean that God chose Mary "before the creation began" and made her the one undamaged specimen of humankind, so that she would be perfectly free to accept the role of being the Mother of God. That was God's initiative. Mary was not chosen because she was good, she was good because she was chosen. The virginal conception of Jesus, the fact that He has no human father, also demonstrates the initiative of God: Jesus was born "not by the will of the flesh nor of the will of man, but of God." (*Jn* 1:13) Those who deny either the Immaculate Conception or the Virginal Conception do not have a specific name, but they *are* heretics for they undermine the whole concept of grace, God's initiative, in effect God's love for us.

Predestination

If Pelagianism is an error on one side, denying the value of grace, the equal and opposite error is *Double Predestination*, which was made manifest in *Calvinism* and *Jansenism*. Both Calvin and Jansen read far too much into the works of St Augustine, who reacted so strongly to Pelagius that he opened the door to the horrible misinterpretation that God predetermines before we are born whether we are to go to heaven or hell, and that there is nothing whatever we can do about it. This of course utterly denies the possibility of love: if we are destined to go to heaven whether we like it or not, we cannot possibly love a God who forces his attentions on us like that, still less can we love a God who has determined we should suffer torment for all eternity for no reason other than that he doesn't feel like saving us. The full horror of double predestination as taught by a strict Calvinist made Wesley exclaim, "what you call god I call the devil!"

Calvinism, as practiced in the Netherlands, South Africa and elsewhere, logically repudiated all sacraments and church ceremonial as irrelevant. Since grace is purely arbitrary, it cannot be conferred by any ceremonial, so there is no point in baptizing infants. Those who refused to baptize infants were originally known in full as *Antipaedobaptists*, shortened first to Anabaptists, and later just Baptists. In their view, Baptism, like the Lord's supper, is only a way of expressing the realization that we are among the elect who are saved.

Jansenism

Jansenism, as practiced in France, less logically retained the whole of Catholic ceremonial, including the sacraments, while depriving them of all meaning. Both Jansenists and Calvinists used the language of grace, but distorted it: a common saying was that "grace is irresistible". If we are chosen to receive grace, then there is nothing we can do which will make us lose it. As a result the most terrible cruelties and vice can flourish in such an environment, though strangely the usual result is extreme Puritanism: the severe restraint of all the baser human emotions, while giving full rein, again, to pride. It was said of the Jansenists that they were "as pure as angels, but as proud as devils". In reality, human nature and conscience cuts in, and very few of those who come from a Calvinist background really hold the full doctrine of double predestination. And by a supreme irony, the usual outcome is actually Pelagianism again: Puritan societies teach that it is up to each one of us to reform our lives by living very strictly according to their code of conduct.

Grace can in fact be resisted: Jesus tells us so in many passages of the gospels, and Judas is the prime example. Mary had to *accept* the call of God: she was totally free to make her choice, but that choice had to be made: "let it be!" (*Lk* 1:38) Her participation in the work of redemption is a necessary part of Catholic doctrine, as yet undefined, for it shows us that each one of us has to make the same act of submission to the grace that God offers

Quietism

This act of submission needs to be made not once but every day. The minor heresy of *Quietism*, part of the reaction to Jansenism, taught that you only need to make a single act of submission to the will of God, and then think no more about it. No, as long as this life lasts we must renew our love for God. As St Paul said, "work out your salvation in fear and trembling; for God is at work in you...not that I have already obtained this or am already perfect." (*Ph* 2:13, 3:12)

Heresy concerning the Nature of the Church

The doctrine of the Catholic Church concerning herself, the discipline of *Ecclesiology*, is a comparatively recent development, and the contradictory heresies have not generally acquired names. However such heresies there certainly are, and as each point of ecclesiology becomes clear, the corresponding heresies emerge.

Unity of the Church

The first, and indeed oldest, doctrine on the nature of the Church is that she is *One*: "I believe in One Holy Catholic and Apostolic Church". Surprisingly, this is now commonly denied, and people frequently talk of "the Churches" in the plural as if Our Lord actually intended there to be many separate and independent churches all teaching different things and practicing different moralities. This is not so, as the Second Vatican Council taught in *Lumen Gentium*. It is the will of God that there be only One Church, one body in Christ. In that sense the word Church has no plural: the word "church" can only be used in the plural (except of course when we just mean buildings) in the rather specialist sense of a "local church", or what we would normally call a diocese. In this sense there are several thousand "churches" within the

One Catholic Church; churches such as the "church of Arundel and Brighton", the "church of Motherwell", the "church of Oudtshoorn", the "church of Uzhgorod". There are also many local churches which we recognize as valid, although not in communion with the One, or necessarily with each other, these are principally the Orthodox churches of the East, so we may talk of the "church of Constantinople", the "church of Thessaloniki", and the "church of Skopje". And then there are other bodies which look like churches but ain't, and these the Council calls "ecclesial bodies". What the Catholic Church finds unacceptable is the idea that there can be "national churches", though the Orthodox seem to have adopted this pattern, and are grouped into "autocephalous churches", manly on national lines, and frequently out of communion with each other, like the "Church of Makedonia" and the adjacent "Church of Greece". The will of God for unity means that we search endlessly for reconciliation with the separated local churches, and we seek the conversion of the "ecclesial bodies". We may not for a moment imagine that the present situation is acceptable, and abandon the quest for true unity.

Church and State

Unity means that the Church is visibly One, united around the Pope as focus of unity and guarantor of truth. As soon as bodies lose contact with the Pope, their integrity begins to disintegrate. The first result is usually subservience to the State. In the East the Orthodox found themselves entirely under the control of the Emperor (the heresy called *Caesaropapism*), leaving them without the freedom to govern themselves, or to make doctrinal decisions without Imperial interference. The corresponding problem in the West is known as *Erastianism*, the subservience of the Church to local kings, archdukes or other princelings. In the modern world it takes the form of subordinating Church order and doctrine to the prevailing fashion of the world, as expressed by ruling Party, legislative assembly, or popular press. There is no particular problem with the Church being recognized by the State, and playing a crucial role in the State, so that having an established Church in itself is not heretical – *antidisestablishmentarianism* is probably not a heresy – but the problem arises when the State starts to dominate the Church, interfering in the appointment of bishops, and enforcing heretical articles of religion as a matter of civil law.

As the authority of national governments weakens, State churches disintegrate. Once people are free to make up their own minds in matters of religion, the former "national churches" splinter into a bewildering number of different denominations. Few of these dare to claim exclusive rights to the truth, for these sects can be numbered in the hundreds of thousands, so effectively what all agree on is that each separate congregation can decide on its own church order, its own teachings and forms of worship. Many of them combine aspects of Christian teaching with animist tradition, developing elaborate ceremonies and impressive costumes, and often with impressively good moral behaviour. Very little remains in common between them and the Catholic Church. But many more of these sects are united in a strange way under a central "evangelical" authority, which exercises a much more efficient control than the poor old Inquisition was ever able to do, and imposes a common body of teaching which they affirm is "Christian" to the exclusion of all other. In fact "evangelical" teaching is nearly all correct as far as it goes: it is heretical only in what it denies, which includes the whole structure of sacraments, the visible Church, and the saints. A common feature among the majority of these small denominations is an obsession with the end of the world, and some bizarre ideas about when and how this is to happen.

What every one of these sects agree about, in fact probably the only point on which they can reach perfect agreement, is repudiation of the Pope. They may be moderately polite to his face, but their whole existence depends on a rejection of the doctrine of the essential unity of the Church around the successor of Peter.

With repudiation of the Papacy usually goes a rejection of the entire hierarchical and sacramental structure of the Catholic Church. Those groups that retain the ministry of bishops and priests usually cannot do so without reference to the Catholic Church, and even the most bizarre little sects may go to strange lengths to establish that their "bishops" have been ordained in a line of succession that goes back to a Catholic bishop. But most denominations are not interested in a sacrificing priesthood at all. They will have ministers under various titles, but do not credit them with any sacramental powers. Various ceremonies may still remain in use, dramatic baptisms in rivers, the laying on of hands, impressive exorcisms, and social suppers, but they are not believed to confer grace. They are seen as ways of expressing the grace that has been given directly by God, or ways of marking stages in a person's growth in holiness, or ways of celebrating fellowship together.

Donatism

The original reason why many groups reject the hierarchy of the Catholic Church goes right back to the fourth century and the heresy of *Donatism*. The Donatists were an African group who were reconstructing the Church after the last and most savage of the ancient persecutions. They believed that a particular bishop had betrayed the Faith during the persecutions by handing over sacred books to the authorities, and because of this betrayal they refused to believe that he retained any power to ordain, or celebrate Mass, or administer the sacraments. Essentially the Donatist heresy was to teach that the personal sins of the priest made his ministry ineffective.

The idea is at first sight attractive. Whenever there are stories about sinful Popes, Bishops, Priests or even Deacons, Donatism re-emerges: people feel that the sacraments administered by these revolting sinners cannot possibly be valid, and that any authority they claim cannot possibly be legitimate. They quote with approval the words of the Gospel, "We know that God does not listen to sinners" (*Jn* 9:31). They fail to notice that these words are on the lips of the Pharisees: Our Lord came to tell us that God does, indeed, listen to sinners, or there would be no hope for any of us. What happens once you embark on Donatism is that all the sacraments become so uncertain that they might as well be abandoned. If personal sin makes a sacrament invalid, that must apply to undisclosed personal sin as well as public scandal. How can anyone be sure that the priest celebrating Mass is not a secret sinner? Or even if he is undoubtedly a man of shining holiness, a real Padre Pio, how can you be sure that the bishop who ordained him was not a secret sinner? Or the bishop who consecrated that bishop? If the line of sacramental power is broken by sin, whether known or secret, then there can be no certainty whatsoever about the validity of any ordination, and consequently the validity of any sacrament. Inevitably you have to move to the position that a sacrament cannot, of itself, confer grace, and that ordination does not confer any powers. The whole structure of church order can be swept away as an irrelevant intrusion.

But of course Donatism doesn't stop with sacramental power: if all authority is forfeit by the sinner, what are we to say of the sinful king? In the ages of faith, when all authority in heaven and on earth was recognized as coming from God, the right of the king to rule was understood as given by God, almost a sacrament. If you deny that the king has this authority because of his personal sins, then you are also denying that he can confer authority on his sheriffs and other officials. Which gives you a marvellous excuse for refusing to pay tax. That is why the kings of Europe were so concerned to stamp out the medieval heresies which had adopted Donatism, such as the Cathars in southern France, or the Lollards in England. They saw heresy as undermining not only the faith of the Church, but also the whole fabric of civil society. Extreme Donatist sects in the end have no alternative but to withdraw from civil society as they had withdrawn from the Church, and to set up isolated communes, living self-sufficient lives remote from the rest of humanity. Less extreme sects content themselves with repudiating the modern Papacy because of stories they love to retail about the Crimes of the Borgia. In fact if you investigate the lives of the Popes from the Borgia family (really *Borja*, they were Spanish), they are disappointingly tame. Certainly there have been Popes, Cardinals and even Deacons who have abused their position to make themselves rich, and whose moral conduct in early life was less than perfect, but not quite on the scale people like to imagine. Nor did their accumulated wealth ever match that of certain modern preachers in sects that have repudiated the Catholic Church.

Our Lady and the Saints

As well as rejecting the earthly hierarchy of the Church, many heresies have also repudiated the heavenly hierarchy, the Saints. It is difficult to see quite why in the sixteenth century there was such violent opposition to the love and respect shown to Our Lady and the Saints, for experience shows that the more devoted we are to Our Lady the closer she will bring us to her Son, whereas if we drive her away from us, we shall soon lose sight of her Son too. Even today most of those who set out to attack the Catholic faith begin by misrepresenting the meaning of Catholic devotion to the saints, and in particular trying to denigrate Our Lady. It is commonplace in Protestantism to deny her any special place in salvation, not only ridiculing the Immaculate

Conception and the Virginal Conception, but asserting that she had many children and was no one special at all. The Gospels themselves will put the record straight, if you only take the trouble to read them carefully. Fundamentally, rejection of Our Lady and the Saints means denying that they are part of the Church, and that the Church continues after death. If we believe that our fellow-Christians can pray for us, and we can ask them to remember us in our prayers, then why should something as trivial as death stop them from praying, us from asking? For we believe that those who have died in Christ are alive with Him, "for He is not God of the dead but of the living." (*Mt* 22:32) The special place of Our Lady is, as we have seen, intrinsic to our understanding of the natures of Jesus. The other Saints, and for that matter the angels, intercede for us because they are fellow-members of the Church, bound to us in the bond of mutual love. How could they refuse us their love, if they are already saturated with the love of God?

Sacraments

The sacraments have always been fertile ground for heresies, beginning with the Cathars who taught that marriage was a sin. It is the Eucharist that has been most often misunderstood, though the rise of the various heresies has been the occasion for corresponding developments in Christian doctrine that have helped us to clarify our understanding of the central role that the Blessed Sacrament takes in our salvation.

Earlier heresies about the sacraments arose from a milder form of Dualism, fuelled by reading too much of the Greek philosopher Plato. Platonism does not go so far as Manicheeism in suggesting there are two gods, but it does suggest that matter is fundamentally a bad thing, and only spirit is of eternal value. In very simple terms, Platonists tend to put everything that exists into one or other camp: on one side are God, angels, and human souls; on the other side are material atoms and anything you care to make out of them. A moment's thought shows how insane this division is. Angels and human souls belong with atoms under the heading of Created Being: God alone is Uncreated. But a subconscious feeling remained that somehow material things did not matter. That meant that bread and wine, water and oil, could not *really* be made holy, and that their use in sacraments could only be symbolic.

The masterly research of St Thomas Aquinas and his contemporaries blew away that cobweb. Beginning with the fundamental premiss that God created all things good, we can see how He takes the material of His creation and uses it as a vehicle of holiness. Objects can indeed be made holy, so that blessed candles, holy water, ashes, palms, and other material things can really be ways of getting in touch

with God. And above all, the material bread and wine of
the Eucharist can really become the Body and Blood of
Christ. To deny that is to deny Creation itself: God spoke,
and it was made, and what He made is good. When God
speaks in the Mass, the bread and wine are remade by that
same creative power. This great development of
understanding in the thirteenth century gave rise
spontaneously to the joyful celebrations of Corpus Christi
and other forms of devotion to the Blessed Sacrament.

Sacramental reality was denied again in the sixteenth
century, by those who refused to read St Thomas and fell
back into Platonic dualism. As a result the Catholic
Church had to clarify her teaching again in the reforming
Council of Trent. But there was still something missing: it
was too easy to see Holy Communion as a private
devotion, only one among various ways of worshipping
God. It was the twentieth century that saw the next
important development of doctrine, and again it was
heresy that triggered it. Certain writers put forward
inadequate ideas about the sacraments, which obscured
the idea that material objects can be sanctified. As a result
there was a massive falling away of faith in the Eucharist,
and it was isolated from its central position in the Church.
This was partly because of the tendency to see the Church
as simply the "people of God". Only in the last days of
Pope John Paul II was this corrected in the masterly

encyclical *Ecclesia de Eucharistia* (2003). The key idea
is that the Church forms the Eucharist, the Eucharist
forms the Church. The Eucharist, like all the sacraments,
belongs within the Church, and can only exist in the
Church, precisely because the Church comes to exist only
through the Eucharist. It is by eating the Body of Christ,
the Eucharist, that we become members of the Body of
Christ, the Church. That of course is how the fundamental
doctrine of salvation works, that is how each of us
individually can "come to share in the divinity of Christ,
who humbled himself to share in our humanity." It can
therefore be seen now as a heresy to deny the place of the
Eucharist in the Church, or to distribute the Eucharist
outside the context of the Church. Here too we see how
we can be in touch with Our Lady and the other Saints:
through Holy Communion we become members of the
Body of Christ and are therefore united with every other
member of the Body of Christ, in this world or the next.

This is all too new for those who deny it to have picked
up a convenient label. It remains to be seen whether late
twentieth-century heretical ideas will survive or not.

A Compendium of all Heresies

Modernism

It will have been noticed that heresies overlap each other, and the same error can affect more than one area of Catholic doctrine, just as every point of Church teaching in some way relates to every other. Yet most heresies of the past picked on one particular point of doctrine, either emphasizing that one to the exclusion of all others, or denying one while still somehow retaining all the others. For a total confusion, the Church had to wait until the end of the nineteenth century, with the rise of *Modernism*. Newman had seen it coming: he declared that the one consistent aim of his life "for thirty, forty, fifty years" had been to resist what he called "Liberalism in matters of religion." By that he meant "the doctrine that there is no positive truth in religion, but that one creed is as good as another. It is inconsistent with any recognition of any religion as *true*." (Biglietto speech, 12th May 1879) All previous heretics, the Arians of the fourth century and the Monophysites of the fifth, the Cathars, the Calvinists, the Jansenists and all the rest, had agreed on the principle that truth is important. They may have been mistaken in what the truth was, but they did want to find and teach the truth. Newman's "liberals" had abandoned the search for truth. By the end of the century what Newman called Liberalism had acquired the label Modernism, meaning that the Church should be continually prepared to change her teaching and practice in order to be "up to date" and "modern". The standard of teaching became, not "is it true?" but "is it trendy?"

Rejection of philosophy

There were two reasons why this came about. The first lay in Luther's rejection of philosophy as a tool for understanding theology. He refused to use the efficient working structure of philosophy that had been built up over the centuries, and insisted that all you needed was faith and an open Bible in order to know the truth. He assumed that his teaching was self-evidently the plain truth of Scripture, not realizing that subconsciously he had come to accept many of the conclusions of long years of philosophical and theological research, such as the doctrine of the Holy Trinity. That doctrine, as we have seen, is by no means self-evident on a first reading of Scripture, and it took the Church three centuries to develop it. "Faith", after Luther, came to mean a blind leap in the dark, accepting propositions without looking at the evidence. In actual experience, for most people "faith" meant accepting what they had been told, without asking questions. Without a basis of sound philosophy and systematic theology, there was no room for discussion or explanation: you either believed what other people had taught you, or you went off and founded a new denomination to make other people believe what you taught. Once it became no longer possible to use military power to keep people together, the result was an ever-increasing number of rival denominations. This led many to conclude that doctrine was simply divisive, and the Church would be better off without any attempt at teaching that anything was really true at all.

Biblical criticism

The second reason was the rise of sceptical Biblical criticism. This began during the eighteenth century (can we not call it the Age of Obfuscation, not "Enlightenment?), and by the late nineteenth century had reached the position we have already described, separating out the "Christ of faith", a purely fictional character, from the "Jesus of History", an inoffensive Jewish rabbi. Therefore they refused to believe that Our Lord ever said to Pilate "I have come into the world to bear witness to the truth" (*Jn* 18:37); they refused to believe there was such a thing as truth, or that it would even be desirable.

The Modernists were never a coherent sect, but a number of scholars who exchanged ideas, and were in some ways amazingly gullible about what was called "the assured result of modern scholarship". These scholars included Lutherans, Anglicans and Catholics, who found common ground in ridiculing the traditional teachings of all denominations. Within the Catholic Church they were comprehensively condemned by St Pius X, who gave Modernism its definition as "a compendium of all heresies", but his rather heavy-handed approach simply drove them underground, to surface in the 1960s. By this time the more intelligent Protestant biblical scholars had come to realize that the Scriptures were much more authentic than the nineteenth-century sceptics had claimed, and the growing evangelical movement led Protestants back to a much more traditional view of Jesus. Unfortunately by the 1970s the sceptical views of the 1890s got into popular publications, and continue to cause considerable confusion among clergy and lay people alike.

The basic principle of adapting Catholic teaching to the mood of the age showed itself in a number of now embarrassing movements. In the 1930s some German Protestants embraced the scientific racial ideas of the period, and adapted their teaching and practice accordingly. In the 1970s some Latin American Catholics embraced the rising tide of Marxism and directed all their catechetical and liturgical efforts to the cause of the Revolution. By the 1990s the trend had become to adapt Catholic moral teaching to the prevailing mood of the press in the more decadent Western countries. In every case, the Modernist approach was to allow the World to set the agenda, and to change the Church to fit in with the ideas of the World.

Fashion

The problem of trying to be always up to date is that you can never quite keep up, and the best efforts to be trendy always seem to be five years behind the times.

The mission of the Church, we should remember, is to "go out and make disciples of all nations" (*Mt* 28:19), not "go and adapt to all nations". Christian teaching must of course take account of the questions of each age, and give an authentically Christian answer to the problems of each nation. That is why a "theology of Liberation" is appropriate, for Christian teachers can and should give moral guidance in accordance with Catholic truth to those who are trying to put right the wrongs of society. But if we stand it on its head and call it "Liberation theology", changing our theology in order to fit in with our preconceived ideas of Marxism-Leninism, then we have ceased to be the teachers of the nations and simply become slaves of fashion. And out of date fashion at that.

The present Holy Father, Benedict XVI, has for many years been drawing our attention to these problems, and encouraging a deeper and more authentic theology, drawing on the rich heritage of the past to answer the vexing questions of the present. The age of Modernism within the Catholic church is now over, though there are still some pockets of resistance to be mopped up. The Catholic Church, it should be stressed, does not forbid the questioning of Catholic doctrine, in fact she positively encourages it. The new *Compendium* to the Catechism is set out precisely as a set of questions which the intelligent Catholic should be asking herself. If you want to go further, the *Summa Theologica* of St Thomas is a series of debates, looking at both sides of every question. Asking questions is the most traditional method of learning the Catholic faith. But if we ask questions we should be prepared to listen to the answers. And if we are not satisfied with the short answers in the *Compendium*, then we are free to read all the works of all the theologians who have ever studied the point. There are no secrets in Catholic teaching. But most peoples' lives are too short to study every point in full depth. For most of us, most of the time, it is sufficient to have the humility to accept that in these matters it is safer to follow the experts, just as we do in medicine, physics or any other science. The heretic is one who is too lazy to find out why the Catholic

Church teaches what she does, and too proud to accept the established teaching if it happens to contradict his private whim.

Truth

Anyone can make honest mistakes, because the range of developed doctrine is now so wide that no one can be an expert in every branch of theology. The Catholic response, when a mistake is pointed out, is to correct it, and make sure that in future any errors are put right. The heretic is one who will not accept correction, but clings to his own ideas even after everyone had shown him how mistaken they are. It is not impossible that I have made mistakes in this pamphlet, though before it is published I hope it will be examined by a competent theologian to check for errors. Any remaining errors will be corrected in the next printing, because it is important to get it right. If in doubt, refer back to the *Catechism of the Catholic Church*. Because we are not supposed to teach our own private opinions, but to convey the truth. Truth is not something which changes from place to place or from time to time. Truth means that which really is, not a lie or an evasion or a compromise. We feel this instinctively whenever we ask any question: we want to know the real answer. If we ask someone how to get to Cape Town, we expect to be put on the right road, and we would be rather angry if someone sent us the wrong way saying, "it doesn't matter, there is no such thing as truth." Or "you shouldn't be hide-bound by conventional ideas of truth." Why then be satisfied if someone tells us the wrong way to get to heaven: can we really say, "it doesn't matter which way you go"?

When someone tell lies about a person we love, we get angry. That is why it is easy for Catholics to get angry when they hear people telling lies about Our Lord, or about Our Lady and the Pope. The proper response of course is not anger but sorrow and patient explanation, but we are only human after all. The truth matters, above all, because it is about someone we love, someone who loves us; indeed Truth is not an abstract concept at all, but a Person, the Person who said, "I am the Way, and the Truth, and the Life" (*Jn* 14:6), and who said, when put on trial for His life, "I have come into the world to bear witness to the truth." (*Jn* 18:37)

The Inquisition

The Inquisition has become a byword for persecution and intolerance, and is often given as a reason for distrusting the Catholic Church. This booklet looks at what led up to this most controversial chapter in the Church's history, what really took place, and what changes led to Pope John Paul II's famous 'apology' in 1997.

ISBN: 978 1 86082 379 4

CTS Code: H 504

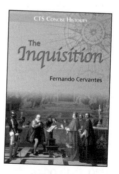

Informative Catholic Reading

We hope that you have enjoyed reading this booklet.

If you would like to find out more about CTS booklets - we'll send you our free information pack and catalogue.

Please send us your details:

Name ....

Address ....

....

....

Postcode ....

Telephone ....

Email ....

Send to: CTS, 40-46 Harleyford Road,
          Vauxhall, London
          SE11 5AY

Tel: 020 7640 0042
Fax: 020 7640 0046
Email: info@cts-online.org.uk